P9-DGV-653

Dec 2014

Dear Readers & Educators,

It is a big world out there, filled with a lot of creatures. While a jellyfish doesn't have a brain to think and reason, our brains have an important role to play in the world.

Our role as humans is to explore, to learn, and to pass on what we know.

The "You Can't" series asks readers to let curiosity, reading, research, and thinking lead to all the possibilities of what we *can* do and be as humans.

You Can't Taste a Pickle with Your Ear
You Can't See Your Bones with Binoculars
You Can't Take Your Body to a Car Mechanic
You Can't Build a House If You're a Hippo
You Can't Spot a Duck in a Desert
You Can't Ride a Bicycle to the Moon
You Can't See a Dodo at the Zoo
You Can't Lay an Egg If You're an Elephant

We would love to know what you have learned from these titles and how you have used it to inspire learning in others.

Visit the "Educators & Librarians" page at **www.blueapplebooks.com** for curriculum and to share your teaching ideas.

You Can't USE YOUR BRAIN If You're a JELLYFISH!

A Book About Animal Brains

by Fred Ehrlich, M.D.

pictures by Amanda Haley

BLUE APPLE

Text copyright © 2005, 2014 by Fred M. Ehrlich
Illustrations copyright © 2005, 2014 by Amanda Haley
All rights reserved
CIP Data is available.
Published in the United States 2014 by
🍎 Blue Apple Books
515 Valley Street, Maplewood, NJ 07040
www.blueapplebooks.com

Printed in China
ISBN: 978-1-60905-454-0
1 3 5 7 9 10 8 6 4 2

Contents

Who has the best brain?

You can't use your brain if you're a jellyfish, because jellyfish don't have brains! Jellyfish can get along without brains. They float along until little fish bump into the stingers on their tentacles and are paralyzed. Then the jellyfish surround these tiny animals and eat them for dinner.

Don't look for the head of a jellyfish.
You can't get in front or behind it.
Go around it until you are dizzy.
If it has a head, you can't find it!

If you didn't have a brain, you'd be in big trouble. Without a brain, you couldn't chew gum or watch television. You couldn't fuss at your parents. You couldn't even breathe.

Your brain is a million times bigger than a mosquito's, 400 times bigger than a crow's, and 20 times bigger than a dog's. Why do you need such a big brain? The answer may surprise you.

We need big brains because we are the most helpless of all animals. We don't have hard shells like cockroaches, or teeth and claws like tigers. We can't dash up trees like squirrels or fly away like birds to get away from danger.

What we do have are minds that can think, and plan, and figure out how to keep ourselves warm and fed and safe. Our brains are what we think with.

The human brain is soft and gray. It is covered with a tough, canvaslike membrane, and it floats in fluid. It is further protected by a skull made of bone. All of this usually keeps our brains safe if we are bumped or hit in the head.

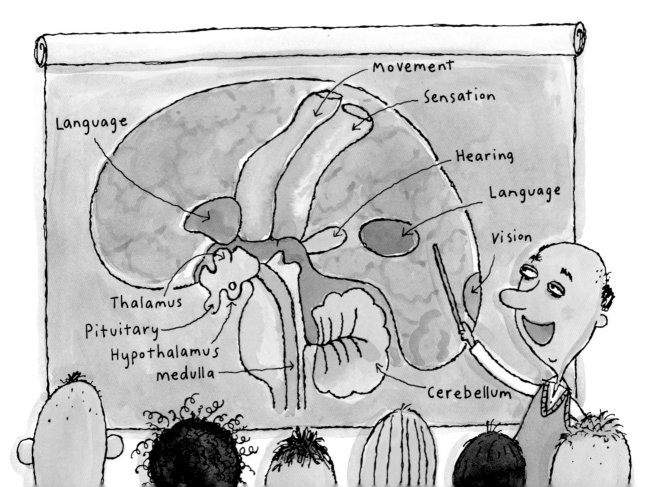

The brain has billions of cells. These cells connect to nerves that run throughout the body. Some of the nerves carry information to the brain from other parts of the body. They tell the brain what the eyes see, what the ears hear, what the nose smells, and what the skin feels. Other nerves carry messages from the brain throughout the body. When you decide to walk, the brain sends messages to your legs, and they move.

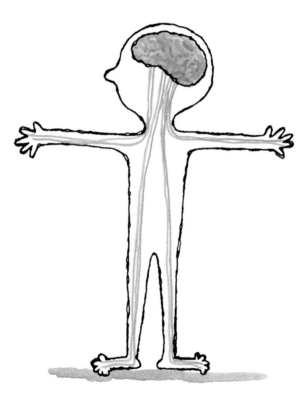

Messages are coming into the brain all the time from the sensory nerves (the nerves that bring information to the brain), and are going out all the time through the motor nerves (the nerves that tell the body how to move). But you are not aware of any of it. You keep your balance and put one foot in front of the other automatically.

What we are aware of are our minds—the part of us that is conscious, that thinks thoughts and feels feelings.

> A body has lots of parts
> Like legs, lungs, and liver.
> A brain tells the body what to do
> So it won't just sit and quiver.

Which animal has the best brain?

A tiger has a proper brain for a tiger; a mosquito has a proper brain for a mosquito; and you have a proper brain for a human being!

Best Brain Contest

I've got a brain. You've got a brain.
Even a mosquito's got a brain.
When I get up in the morning, gonna use my brain
And start thinking.

I've got a brain. You've got a brain.
Even my kitten's got a brain.
When I get ready for school, gonna use my brain
And keep thinking.

I've got a brain. You've got a brain.
Everyone at school's got a brain.
When I get to school, gonna use my brain
And keep on thinking.

I've got a brain. You've got a brain.
Everyone at home's got a brain.
When it gets dark, gonna turn down my brain
And start dreaming.

I've got a brain. You've got a brain.
Even a mosquito's got a brain.
When I get up in the morning, gonna use my brain
And start thinking.

CHAPTER ONE
Small Animals, Small Brains

Small animals such as insects and worms have small brains. Our brains are much larger, not only because our bodies are bigger, but also because our brains have a thick outer layer called the cerebral cortex. This layer is largely responsible for dealing with language and thought.

Insects and the "lower" animals have very thin cerebral cortexes, or none at all. They don't need to think like humans do.

> Animal brains
> Have different shapes,
> From little to big,
> From bugs to apes.

Worm Brains

Worms have one of the least complicated brains. Their brains have 302 nerve cells. In contrast, the human brain has 100,000,000,000 (100 billion) nerve cells.

A helminthologist, a scientist who studies worms, once said, "Because there are so few cells in worms' brains, it makes it easier to study how they work. What I learn about worm brains helps me understand human brains."

As small as a worm's brain is, it can do some things that ours can't. Worms specialize in chemotaxis, the ability to detect certain chemicals in the environment.

When you are hungry, you have to think about where food is and how to get there. Worms just wander about in the soil until they detect food by chemotaxis. This does not involve thinking.

Through the dirt a little wormy
Tunnels tunnels. Squirmy squirmy.
It has no legs. It has no feet.
Still it finds enough to eat!

Mosquito Brains

Mosquitoes have brains about the size of the period at the end of this sentence. Yet, they can

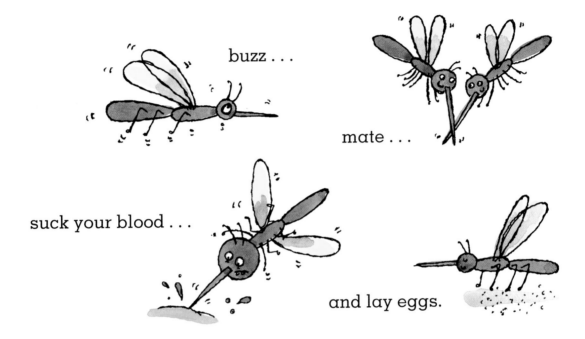

buzz . . .

mate . . .

suck your blood . . .

and lay eggs.

They do all of this unconsciously, or by instinct. That is, their brains are constructed so that they automatically react to their environments. They do not have to learn and make decisions the way humans do.

If your little brother bites you, it is not instinct. He could decide not to bite you. A mosquito can't.

Mosquito brains are tiny,
But mosquitoes do not care.
They buzz around my ears all night
And bite me everywhere.

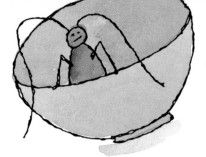

Cockroach Brains

The cockroach doesn't have much of a brain either. It has three collections of nerve cells called ganglia that do the work of a brain. One ganglion is for seeing, one controls the cockroach's antennae, and one is for everything else.

Cockroaches do many of the things that people do. They walk around; they find food; they hide from danger; they find other cockroaches and reproduce. But all cockroaches are pretty much the same. We do not speak of smart and stupid cockroaches. Cockroaches do not think. They do everything by instinct.

It's true that cockroaches
Cannot think.
They never learn to
Keep out of the sink!

CHAPTER TWO
Bigger Animals, Bigger Brains

Birds, Cats, and Dogs

Birds, cats, and dogs are vertebrates. Vertebrates are animals with backbones. They include everything from mice to monkeys, from salmon to sparrows. The backbone protects the spinal cord. The spinal cord contains the nerves that carry messages to and from the brain.

Vertebrates evolved later than invertebrates (animals without backbones) such as jellyfish and cockroaches. We say they are more advanced because they are more like us.

Bird Brains

If being smart means getting good grades in school, then birds are dumb. But if it means surviving in the world, then they are smart. Birds have to find food to eat and safe places to sleep. They also must find mates, build nests, and raise their chicks so that there will be more birds in the future.

All bird brains are not the same. If you put the brain of a crow on top of a hummingbird, the hummingbird could not get off the ground. A ruby-throated hummingbird weighs only about three grams. A crow weighs 150 times more—about 450 grams.

Crows and hummingbirds have brains that tell their wings what to do so that they don't fall out of the sky. Crows can only fly forward. Hummingbirds can fly forward or backward, or just hold still in the air.

Hummingbirds hold still,
Here and there,
In the middle
Of the air.

Hawks and Owls

Different birds live differently, and their brains are suited to what they have to do. Hawks have excellent eyesight. From high in the sky they can see a mouse in a meadow. The hawk's brain recognizes the mouse as something good to eat. It then tells the body to dive and catch it.

Owls also hunt mice. But owls hunt at night because they have excellent night vision.

A hawk sees a mouse
While flying up high.
It dives for its dinner
Right out of the sky.

Crows

Crows are among the most adaptable of birds. This suggests that they are among the most intelligent as well, since they learn how to live in many different situations.

Crows can live close to people. They have a good sense of danger so they can learn to get out of the way. They are also omnivores. They can eat everything from seeds and nuts to worms and small birds that they kill, as well as dead animals of any size. This means they can find enough to eat almost anywhere, from forests and fields to garbage dumps and highways.

Crows can't speak in words, but they make many different sounds that have meaning to other crows. They learn some of these sounds when they are chicks. Just like people who learn different accents from the speech they hear, crow sounds are different in different parts of the world.

Pet Birds

A bird's ability to learn makes it an appealing pet to many people. Birds get to know the people who take care of them. They may become so attached to one person that they will attack other people who get too close. This may resemble the behavior that birds need when they live in the wild, where they must protect their families from other animals.

Pet birds can also be taught to land on a person's hand. This takes repeated training and patience by the owner. When the birds get it right, they are rewarded with a treat, such as a piece of chopped up caterpillar. Yuck!

Different birds have different talents. Parrots and some other birds can be taught to say words. This is not the same as the speech that a human baby starts to learn. The baby soon learns the meaning of different words and puts them together to say things. The parrot just imitates and repeats.

Dog and Cat Brains

Some people think dogs and cats are one step up from birds and fish because they are more like humans. But it's better to think of an animal as sideways instead of "up" or "down." Every animal has its own place in the environment; each has a brain perfectly suited to what it must do.

Dogs and cats have been domesticated. This means they have been bred from wild animals in order to live with people as pets and companions, or work for us as seeing-eye dogs or guard dogs. They can be trained to pee and poop in special places.

It is easier to teach dogs than cats. This is more because of their backgrounds and personalities than because of their intelligence. For example, cats descended from solitary hunters, while dogs' ancestors hunted in packs. This makes dogs better suited to fitting in with a group and following rules. Cats prefer to do things on their own.

Dogs follow rules.
Cats aren't like that.
Just try to train
A seeing-eye cat!

What Your Dog Can Learn

Border Collies compete in a sort of doggie Super Bowl. Following its owner's whistle and voice commands, a dog has to locate a group of sheep on a hillside 600 yards away, bring the sheep to the competition area, and drive them through a series of gates and into a pen. These dogs are really smart.

In a sense, the dogs have also trained their owners. The owner has to give only those commands that the dog can understand and follow. A dog's owner who doesn't really understand the dog will end up making it run in circles and look miserable.

My dog's name is Flick.
I've taught him a trick.
He catches—I toss.
Now he thinks he's the boss!

What Your Cat Can Learn

Cats are loners. They hunt by themselves and take care of themselves. They sometimes act as if they are doing you a favor by living with you. If you get to know them, you may gradually become real friends, but it takes time and patience.

Watch a cat's tail. It says a lot:

1) Tail hanging down:
    "All is well."

2) Tail straight up:
    "Let's be friends."

3) Tail stiff and curved
    with hair standing up: "Watch out!"

Both you and the cat must have pretty complicated brains to be able to understand each other.

CHAPTER THREE

Monkeys, Apes, and Other Primates

Primate Brains

Primates are a class of animals that includes monkeys, apes, baboons, gorillas, chimpanzees, orangutans, and humans. For primates, vision is more important than smell. This means that the parts of the brain that have to do with sight are bigger, and those related to smell are smaller.

Communication among primates is more complex than among insects and birds. Although they are not able to use words as humans do, all other primates communicate nonverbally with hand gestures, facial expressions, and body movements.

hungry   relaxed   fearful

People who study chimpanzees can tell when they are sad,
lonely, angry, hungry, hurt, or content.

They can often predict what a chimp is about to do.
This chimp is not about to attack;
he is just being friendly.

Monkeys and apes,
Gorillas and chimps,
All of their little ones
Are cuddly imps.

Gorilla Brains

Gorillas are the biggest and strongest of the primates. The males are often six feet tall and can weigh up to 450 pounds. For their size, however, their brains are not as big as those of the much smaller chimpanzees.

Gorillas are like humans in a number of ways. They live in families and may form tribes with 40 or more members. They make mattresses of branches and leaves on which they sleep at night.

A gorilla beats
His hairy chest
To tell the world
He is the best.

Monkey Brains

"New World monkeys" are monkeys that live in the Western hemisphere. Almost all have prehensile tails (tails that can grasp things by wrapping around them). This is important because they live high up in trees in the jungle, where they use their tails for swinging from branch to branch and for climbing. As you might guess, their brains have a well-developed section devoted to just controlling their tails.

"Old World monkeys" are monkeys that live in the Eastern hemisphere. Mother monkeys do a lot of teaching. For weeks, a mother tastes every scrap of food that her baby puts in its mouth, teaching it what is and is not safe to eat. The young monkey has to be taught to climb and practices on lower, safer branches. Old World monkeys do not have prehensile tails.

A mother monkey also disciplines her child by grabbing the young monkey by its ear or neck and slapping it.

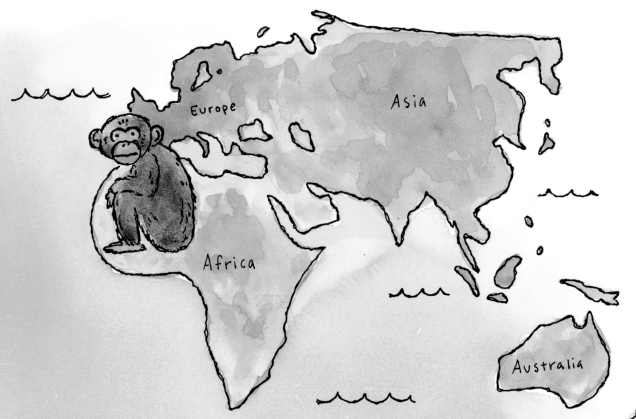

East is East and West is West.
Monkey mommies know what's best.

Chimpanzee Brain

A chimpanzee's body is similar to ours. If you don't think so, just compare a chimp's body to a tiger or a whale's body! A chimp's brain is also similar to ours. Although it weighs only about one pound (our brain weighs about three-and-a-half pounds), its structure is very much like ours. And it has a thick cerebral cortex, the part of the brain involved in thinking.

It is clear from watching chimps that they can think. But they cannot use language for thinking the way we do. Some of our thinking occurs through pictures in our minds, and chimps may well be able to think that way. But most of our thinking uses words. If this is not clear, just try thinking without using words.

I never heard a chimp complain
It wasn't happy with its brain,
Or felt on some days like a fool,
Like I do when I'm late for school.

Using language to think gives us a big advantage. We can learn not only from how our families and friends act, but from what they say.

We can say, "I can't give you an answer right now. I have to stop and think about it." Through books, we can learn from people whom we have never met. Chimps can't do that.

There are many things that chimps have to be taught. Baby chimps watch their parents getting termites to eat. The parents use one kind of stick to poke holes in termite nests and another kind of stick to fish the termites out. It takes practice for the young ones to be able to do this.

A chimp can stand up
To see what's around.
It can look in the trees
And look at the ground.

It can see where it's going
And try not to slip.
But it can't study geography,
Or plan a big trip.

CHAPTER FOUR
The Biggest Primate Brain of All

The Human Brain

The things our brains can do make us the only primates that can live in every part of the world. We are not the biggest, the strongest, or the fastest, but we can change the world in ways that make it safe for us. Our brains help us to survive.

We build shelters to protect us; we make clothing that we can take on and off; we farm, hunt, fish, and raise animals for food. We have learned to live in most places in the world, from the hottest to the coldest, from the driest to the wettest, and from the highest to the lowest.

Animals cannot fix the world to suit them, except in small ways such as building nests or digging burrows.

Babies' Brains

At birth a human baby's brain can make its body do all the things it needs to do to survive as long as there are adults to take care of the baby. It can suck to get milk. It can get rid of waste as urine (pee) and feces (poop). It can cry to make its parents and others pay attention to it.

The baby's brain also regulates things such as breathing, digesting, and keeping the body's temperature even. These functions go on throughout life without our being aware of them unless something goes wrong.

Newborns can only focus up to 8-12 inches away (handy for learning to recognize mom or dad!), but the baby's other senses are well developed at birth.

A baby's brain, however, is not able to do the many things that it will have to do later. It is immature. It needs to grow more cells and make more connections among the cells before it can send the signals to sit up, then stand, then walk and talk, and then get into trouble.

It may seem odd to think of getting into trouble as an achievement. But we can get into trouble only when we are capable of telling the difference between right and wrong, and it takes a more mature brain to do this. It makes no sense to punish small babies.

You can't sing songs.
You can't stand up.

You can't play ball,
Or hold a cup.

But wait a while
And you will get it.

In the meantime,
Just don't sweat it!

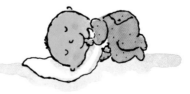

Computers Do Not Have Brains

"Can computers be more intelligent than we are?"
This question was asked a lot after the computer Deep Blue won a chess game against the world's best player. The answer depends on the difference between being "smart" (quick and able to keep track of a lot of things at once) and being "intelligent" (having sound judgment and the ability to reason).

Computers can be smarter than we are since they can keep track of much more data and calculate much faster than we can. But they are not more intelligent. They were built. We were born. We started out little and had to learn everything we could about the world.

We had to grow up little by little. We know what it feels like to have our feelings hurt and what it feels like to hurt someone else's feelings. Computers can never learn these things, because they have no brains, no minds, and no feelings.

"I'm a computer. I'm smarter than you."

"But you can't build me like I built you!"

Science and the Brain

For thousands of years, people have been interested in how the mind works. But first they needed to figure out that the brain is the part of the body that is responsible for the conscious mind.

Long ago, doctors discovered that if the brain was injured, people could not do things they had been able to do before. They noticed that injuries to the same parts of brains in different people caused the same problems.

Scientists studied the brains of people who had died. They described what the inside of the brain looked like. They also studied animal brains and began to figure out what parts of the brain controlled different functions.

Later, X-rays and electroencephalographs (machines that record the electrical activity of the brain) made it possible to study people's brains while they were still alive.

One of the hardest things that people are trying to understand about the brain is how a part of the body, made only of flesh and blood, can produce a "mind." The mind gives us thinking, memory, and feelings. But the mind is not located in any one part of the brain the way seeing or hearing is. It depends on the whole brain working together.

Speaking

Vision

hearing

movement

Feeling

Mosquitoes operate like tiny machines. They exist, but they don't really know they exist. They don't have fond memories. They don't feel happiness or sorrow.

Chimpanzees, on the other hand, are clearly aware of themselves. They form friendships. They feel happy and sad. They have brains, and they also have minds!

In the last few years, we have made great progress in the ability to study living brains. Using new technology, scientists can see what part of the brain is most active when a person is doing arithmetic, humming a tune, or feeling afraid.

My mind is where I keep my secrets.
My brain is where I keep my mind.
If you could see what I am thinking,
You'd be surprised at what you'd find.

CONCLUSION

Human beings can think about how their brains work. That is what we are doing right now. We are the only animals that can do this. Other animals survive by adapting to the world as they find it. We change the world to make it safe and comfortable for us.

Our three-and-a-half-pound brains do astonishing things. Not only do they let us find food and keep out of danger, but they make it possible for us to have minds—minds that can think about the past and imagine the future; minds that can solve complicated problems.

We know that after the warmth of summer comes the cold of winter, so we build houses and make warm clothes. We know that after the fruits, nuts, and grains of autumn come the snows of winter when nothing grows, so we preserve and store up food.

One person alone could never figure all this out. It takes many people living over many years to observe that seasons happen every year. Someone who has lived through many winters can tell a child, "The nights are getting longer and the days are getting colder, but long, warm days will be back again."

A cat stretched out purring in the sun must know something about being happy and even perhaps about recognizing beauty.

But we are the ones who sing songs and write poetry and paint pictures. We may not be the only animals that feel love, but we are the only ones who say, "I love you."

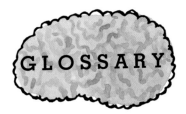

GLOSSARY

cerebral cortex: the thick outer layer of the brain that is largely responsible for dealing with language and thought

chemotaxis: the ability to detect certain chemicals in the environment

consciously: doing something and being aware of it

domesticated: animals bred to live with people as pets

ganglia: collections of nerve cells that do the work of a brain

helminthologist: a scientist who studies worms

instinct: an inborn pattern of activity that is a response to the environment

invertebrate: an animal without a backbone

motor nerves: the nerves that tell the body how to move

nonverbal: without words

omnivores: animals that can eat both other animals and plants

prehensile: able to grasp things by wrapping around them

primate: a member of a class of animals that includes monkeys, apes, chimpanzees, orangutans, and humans

sensory nerves: the nerves that bring information to the brain

unconsciously: doing something without being aware of it

vertebrate: an animal with a backbone